Private Edwin E. Jennison, a Confederate soldier in a Georgia regiment

Union Sergeant Oscar Ryder, a Union soldier in the 7th New York State militia

The Battle of Shiloh is depicted in this Currier and Ives print. The figures on horseback in the foreground are some of the Union generals who directed the battle. From left to right: Thomas Crittenden, Lew Wallace, Don Carlos Buell, William T. Sherman, and Ulysses S. Grant.

Cornerstones of Freedom

The Story of
THE
BATTLE OF SHILOH

By Zachary Kent

J
973.731
K

CHILDRENS PRESS®
CHICAGO

This view of the Battle of Shiloh was drawn by a Confederate soldier.

Library of Congress Cataloging-in-Publication Data

Kent, Zachary.

The story of the Battle of Shiloh / by Zachary Kent.
    p.   cm. — (Cornerstones of freedom)
    Summary: Describes the second great battle of the Civil
War, the Battle of Shiloh, at the time the bloodiest battle
fought on American soil.
    ISBN 0-516-04754-X
    1. Shiloh, Battle of, 1862—Juvenile
literature. [1. Shiloh, Battle of, 1862. 2. United
States—History—Civil War, 1861-1865—
Campaigns.] I. Title. II. Series.
E473.54.K46   1991
973.7'31—dc20   90-21646
                                     CIP
                                     AC

Ulysses S. Grant

Black smoke poured from the stacks of the steamboat *Tigress* as it hurried up the Tennessee River on the morning of April 6, 1862. On deck, Union Major General Ulysses S. Grant grimly gazed ahead. As the boat approached Pittsburg Landing, Tennessee, Grant saw thousands of blue-clad soldiers crouching in panic along the muddy riverbank.

Less than two miles away, a furious battle raged. Thundering cannon shook the earth. Cracking muskets sent bullets whistling through the trees. As the firing drew closer, some frightened men hugged the muddy ground. Others splashed into the water and tried to swim to safety. One Yankee witness later said, "Such . . . terror and confusion I never saw before and do not wish to see again."

At dawn, charging Confederate troops had launched a surprise attack against the Union army encamped at Pittsburg Landing. As the screaming Rebels smashed past the Union guards, many startled Yankees had abandoned their tents and

General Grant at the Battle of Shiloh

campfires. They retreated, running through the woods all the way to the Tennessee River.

The minute his boat reached the landing, General Grant rode his horse ashore. Determined to save his army, he immediately ordered ammunition sent to the men still fighting at the front. Then he called for badly needed reinforcements. That done, Grant spurred his horse forward into the thick of the fight.

At the battlefront, Grant discovered the fight raging with savage fury. Near a crude log church called the Shiloh Meeting House, cannonballs shrieked through the air. In dense woods and tangled underbrush, Confederate bayonets flashed

6

and Union rifle volleys blazed. Most of these soldiers had never been in combat before, but they fought with uncommon valor and brutal stubbornness. When the American Civil War was over, few people would disagree with General Grant. "Shiloh," he would gravely declare, "was the severest battle fought at the West during the war."

For over forty years, the question of slavery had pushed the United States toward civil war. In the North, thousands of European immigrants worked in thriving factories. Across the Northern states, railroads carried goods from one industrial city to another. Most Northerners had no use for slavery and many considered it to be cruel and immoral.

A busy Northern factory in 1865

Slaves (left) picking cotton in Southern fields. An ad (right) for a Charleston, South Carolina, store advertises the store's clothes while crusading at the same time against the election of Abraham Lincoln.

In the South, however, cotton was the major crop, and it was grown on large plantations worked by African slaves. The Southerners depended on slavery for the success of their farming economy.

The problem reached a crisis point when Abraham Lincoln was elected sixteenth president of the United States in November 1860. Angry Southerners feared that Lincoln, a Northerner from Illinois, planned to abolish slavery. They insisted the federal government had no right to force laws upon the Southern states.

One by one, eleven Southern states—South Carolina, Mississippi, Florida, Alabama, Georgia, Louisiana, Texas, Virginia, Arkansas, Tennessee, and North Carolina—left the Union. These states formed the Confederate States of America and elected Jefferson Davis president. In April 1861, Confederate cannon bombarded Fort Sumter, a Union fort in the harbor of Charleston, South Carolina, and the Civil War began.

The surrender of Fort Sumter shocked Northerners. In Washington, D.C., President Lincoln called

Jefferson Davis (left) and Abraham Lincoln (right) were the opposing war leaders. A Confederate flag flies above a heavily damaged Fort Sumter after the surrender.

Bounty money was given to men who joined the Union army. "Bounty jumpers" would enlist, desert, and then join again in a different state to collect another bounty.

for volunteers to put down the rebellion and vowed to hold the United States together at all costs. Across the South, Confederates loudly cheered their first victory. Many Southerners looked upon the coming conflict as a second war of independence.

War fever gripped the nation. Eager men and boys joined army companies and regiments. At the start of the Civil War, Ulysses S. Grant was almost thirty-nine years old. He was a clerk in his father's leather-goods store in Galena, Illinois. Grant's military education at West Point and his Mexican War experience, however, earned him a

10

brigadier general's commission. Soon, the U.S. War Department placed him in command of a Union army of 17,000 men in southern Illinois.

In February 1862, U.S. Navy gunboats captured Fort Henry on the Tennessee River in Tennessee. Marching swiftly, Grant's troops next surrounded nearby Fort Donelson on the Cumberland River. Hard fighting kept the Confederate troops trapped inside. Soon white flags fluttered in response to Grant's blunt demand for "unconditional and immediate surrender." A Confederate army of close to 14,000 men marched out in surrender.

Ulysses S. Grant (left, on horseback) attacks Fort Donelson.

Throughout the North, citizens wildly celebrated the stunning captures of Fort Henry and Fort Donelson, claiming that Grant's initials, U.S., stood for "Unconditional Surrender." Eager for further victories, Congress rewarded Grant with a promotion to major general. During the next few weeks, the Union army pushed south to clear the last of the Confederate troops out of western Tennessee. The important railroad junction at Corinth, Mississippi, was Grant's next objective. While he prepared to attack, most of his men were encamped at Pittsburg Landing, twenty-two miles away.

The Union camps rested on high bluffs on the west bank of the Tennessee River. Deep ravines and small streams twisted through parts of this rugged countryside. In some places, farmers had cleared the dense forest and planted fields and orchards. A rough, one-room log church stood in an open spot. This Methodist meeting house was called Shiloh—a Biblical name meaning "place of peace."

Most of the 42,000 Yankees gathered near Pittsburg Landing in early April 1862 were new recruits. Drill sergeants barked orders as they marched these inexperienced soldiers in formation and taught them how to shoot muskets. "The boys are getting anxious for a fight," one Iowa soldier, Alexander Downing reported.

Fifty-nine-year-old General Albert Sidney Johnston commanded the Confederate soldiers in the West. He desperately gathered some 40,000 men at Corinth, Mississippi. To hold off the Yankee advance, officers quickly tried to teach their raw troops how to function as an army. On April 2, however, word reached Corinth that Union major general Don Carlos Buell was marching 30,000 soldiers west from Nashville, Tennessee. Clearly, the Confederates must act before Buell's troops could unite with General Grant's army. "Now is the moment to advance and strike the enemy at Pittsburg Landing," insisted General P.G.T. Beauregard, Johnston's second in command. General Johnston agreed.

By the evening of April 5 the Confederate army

Confederate General Albert Sidney Johnston (left) was killed at Shiloh. Major General Don Carlos Buell (center) led 30,000 Union troops. General P. G. T. Beauregard (right) became the Confederate commander after the death of Johnston.

lay hidden in the woods two miles south of the Union camps. "Gentlemen, we shall attack at daylight," Johnston told his division commanders.

Long before dawn on April 6, Union soldiers scouting along the paths south of Pittsburg Landing suddenly were fired upon by the leading regiments of the Confederate attack. Quickly they rushed back to their camps to warn their comrades. One wounded soldier staggered among the tents of the 53rd Ohio Regiment. "Get in line!" the soldier shouted. "The Rebels are coming!"

Bugles blared as sleepy men threw off their blankets and grabbed their guns. Just as the sun's first rays filtered through the woods, division commander Brigadier General William T. Sherman saw hundreds of shining bayonets thrusting through the thick underbrush. "My God, we are attacked!" the general exclaimed.

Bullets ripped through the trees, and with piercing shouts, the Rebels charged. Cannon boomed in every clearing. Confederate infantrymen rapidly loaded and fired their muskets. Riding among his gray-clad soldiers, General Johnston promised, "Tonight we will water our horses in the Tennessee."

Confusion swept through the Union ranks as the Yankee troops were driven back. Many panicked soldiers fled. "The main thing was to get out of there

14

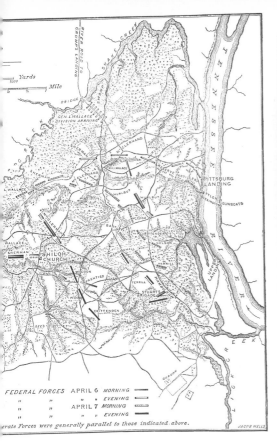

This "official" map of the Battle of Shiloh (left) accompanied an article about the battle by General Grant (above) that was published in *The Century* magazine in 1885.

as quick as we could," admitted Illinois Private Leander Stillwell. Wounded and frightened troops clogged the roads as they retreated to the river landing. "We're whipped, we're whipped; we're all cut to pieces!" yelled a retreating colonel.

Some fresh regiments tried to advance through the crowd to support the Union line. Along the crumbling Yankee front, officers shouted frantic orders. Wounded men screamed in pain, and gunsmoke choked the air. Many brave Northern regiments tried to hold their positions, but the Rebels swarmed among them and the Union line repeatedly fell back.

At the center of the Union line, the Confederates swept into the hastily abandoned camps of Brigadier General Benjamin Prentiss's division. Grinning Rebels gobbled down the Yankee breakfasts they found cooking. Others ransacked tents and baggage before moving on.

Nine miles downriver, General Grant sat at his headquarters in the village of Savannah. As he lifted a cup of coffee to his lips, the Union commander heard the distant rumble of cannon. "Gentlemen," he declared to his staff, "the ball is in motion. Let's be off." As the *Tigress* neared Pittsburg Landing, a scene of complete confusion greeted Grant. Thousands of horrified Yankees crowded shoulder to shoulder at the water's edge.

Union troops at Pittsburg Landing.

Major General Lew Wallace (left). Confederate troops (above) capture Union headquarters and artillery batteries on the first day of the Battle of Shiloh.

Instantly Grant began issuing orders. One staff officer galloped five miles north to Crump's Landing, calling upon Major General Lew Wallace to send reinforcements at once. Another messenger hurried across the river with orders that General Buell's approaching army make haste to reach the battlefield as soon as possible.

Within minutes, Grant himself was riding to the front. Smoking a cigar, he calmly moved among his fighting troops. "During the whole of Sunday," he later explained, "I was continuously engaged in passing from one part of the field to another, giving directions to division commanders."

Major General Benjamin Prentiss (above).
Brigadier General William T. Sherman (right)

Near the Shiloh church, Grant found General Sherman, covered with dust, a bandage wrapped around a buckshot wound through his hand. Fearlessly, Sherman believed his division could hold on if given more shells and cartridges. Grant promised him the ammunition and then went to see General Prentiss at the center of the Union line. Prentiss's men had been pushed back a mile from their campground, but these Yankees were stoutly resisting all enemy attacks, crouching along a sunken road. Grant commanded Prentiss to hold his position at all costs.

18

General Grant rode from one part of the battlefield to another, directing the battle.

Throughout the late morning and early afternoon, the bloody fight continued. Relentlessly, the gray-clad Confederates kept up their attacks on the wavering Union line. "Tell Beauregard that we are sweeping the field before us and I think we shall press them to the river," declared General Johnston to one staff officer. The Rebels now believed they could destroy the Union army. "We were crowding them..." Tennessee soldier Sam Watkins later recalled. "We were jubilant; we were triumphant.... The Federal dead and wounded covered the ground."

During the afternoon, the fighting roared most fiercely in the woods and fields along the Sunken Road. The brave Yankees commanded by General Prentiss refused to budge another inch. Soon the bullets flew so fast that the soldiers called the awful place the "Hornet's Nest." One Confederate brigade after another hurled themselves forward. The dead and injured dropped to the ground in bloody heaps. Here and there, rifle flashes set the woods on fire.

A flowering peach orchard stood in front of one section of the Sunken Road. Bullets ripped through the blossoms until the petals fluttered down like confetti. "I will lead you," General Johnston shouted to a Rebel brigade preparing to charge among the peach trees. With a wild yell, the Confederates rushed forward. In the attack, a Yankee bullet ripped the sole from one of Johnston's boots and other bullets nicked his uniform. But the fierce Confederate general remained unhurt.

Soon afterward, Johnston rode into a nearby woods. Suddenly, a bullet thudded into his right leg behind his knee. The general's face turned pale as an aide helped him from his horse. Blood poured from the wound and formed a puddle on the ground. Johnston's staff surgeon was away treating other wounded men and no one thought to tie a tourniquet tightly around the leg. The bullet had cut an

The battle at the peach orchard (above). Map of the routes by which the Union army was reinforced at Shiloh (below left). General Grant in the field (below right)

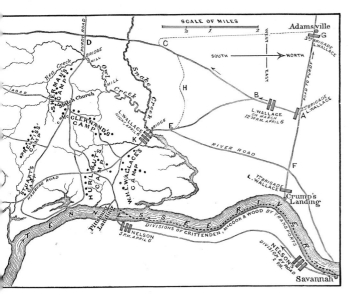

artery—and in a few minutes the gallant Confederate commander bled to death.

The death of Johnston at around 2:30 P.M. left General Beauregard in charge of the Confederate troops. By that time, both the left and right flanks of the Union line had sagged back toward the river. Only the stubborn fighters in the Hornet's Nest kept the Rebels from sweeping the Yankees into the river. To break this stronghold in the center of the Union line, Confederate Brigadier General Daniel Ruggles wheeled sixty-two cannon into position side by side. As these guns erupted in a fiery bombardment, cannonballs crashed into the earth within the Hornet's Nest, sending dirt and mangled bodies flying. Stunned Yankees hugged the ground as shrieking Confederate artillery shells splintered the tree branches overhead.

At last this hail of iron proved too great. The Rebels were closing in, and soon General Prentiss discovered that the Hornet's Nest was completely surrounded. Late in the afternoon, the courageous general surrendered the remaining 2,200 men of his battered division.

"Cease firing! White flag!" yelled the jubilant Confederate officers.

Many Rebels cheered when they saw the captured Yankees being herded to the rear. They believed the

loss of the Hornet's Nest meant the Union army was beaten. As evening fell, General Beauregard sent a telegram to the Confederate capital at Richmond, Virginia. "After a severe battle of ten hours..." he exclaimed, "we gained a complete victory, driving the enemy from every position."

Pushed to the edge of the river, the shaken Union army seemed on the verge of total defeat. Grimly, General Grant formed a new defensive line. He plugged gaps with men from broken regiments and bands of stragglers. He ordered Colonel J. D. Webster to place every piece of cannon he could find

A Confederate brigade charges Union troops in the Hornet's Nest.

23

Union gunboats at Pittsburg Landing on the evening of the first day of the battle

on high ground behind a creek called the Dill Branch. On the Tennessee River, two U.S. Navy gunboats, the *Lexington* and the *Tyler*, sent shells crashing among the Rebels in the distant woods.

It was after dark when Union general Lew Wallace finally reached the field with 5,000 men from Crump's Landing. Grant ordered these fresh troops to support the right side of the Union line. Across the Tennessee River, the first of General Buell's soldiers at last arrived. Steamboats ferried the regiments across the water to Pittsburg Land-

24

ing. With their bands blaring, the soldiers marched ashore. They gasped in surprise at the thousands of Yankees swarming along the riverbank. Brigadier General William Nelson led his troops through the mob of stragglers. "If you won't fight," he roared, "get out of the way, and let men come here who will!" It had been a very bad day for the Union army at Shiloh, but perhaps now they could hold on.

During the night, a cold rain fell as artillery shells still crashed among the trees. Dazed soldiers wandered through the woods. Dead and dying men

Union wounded and stragglers on the way to the landing pass an ammunition wagon going to the front.

covered the ground. At the Peach Orchard, many wounded men crawled to the edge of a nearby pond, desperate for water. The water turned so red with the blood of the wounded that the place became known as "Bloody Pond."

Weary from long hours of fighting, General Sherman found his friend General Grant huddled beneath a tree in the rain. "Well, Grant," he remarked, "we've had the devil's own day, haven't we?"

"Yes," the Union commander quietly answered, puffing hard on his cigar. "Yes. Lick 'em tomorrow, though."

General Grant refused to consider defeat, and his tough attitude greatly impressed his men. Through the stormy night, broken regiments re-formed, and fresh troops continued to ferry across the river.

At dawn on April 7, Grant gave the order to his generals, ". . . advance and recapture our original camps." With a roar, the Yankee soldiers charged over the muddy, bloody ground and smashed into the Rebel positions.

Now it was the Confederate army's turn to be surprised. General Beauregard had expected the beaten Yankees to retreat northward under cover of darkness. Stunned by the idea of a second day's fight, the tired rebels reloaded their rifles.

At the end of the first day of the battle, the Union troops (above) took up a final defensive position on a ridge above Pittsburg Landing, and spent a long, miserable, night in the rain (below right). The map (below left) shows the positions of the Union troops throughout the battle.

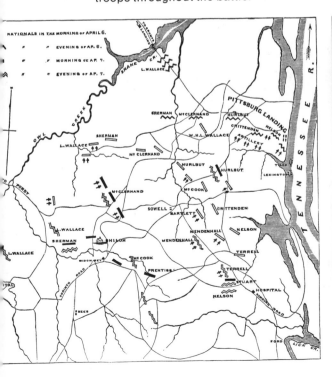

Confederate Brigadier General Patrick Cleburne (left). The painting (left) depicts the Confederate line of battle on the second day, "with fate against them."

Fierce Confederate countercharges could not halt the advancing Yankees. "My men were dropping all around before the fire of an unseen foe," exclaimed Rebel Brigadier General Patrick Cleburne. Storms of bullets whizzed through the trees and thickets as the battle swirled in mad confusion. Grimly the Yankees pressed ahead. Greatly outnumbered now, the Rebel line wavered and cracked in the early afternoon. Many exhausted Confederates fled the field, dropping guns and knapsacks as they ran.

"General, do you not think our troops are ... ready to dissolve?" asked Confederate Staff Officer Thomas Jordan.

28

General Beauregard recognized the growing danger to his army. "I intend to withdraw in a few moments," he gravely responded.

By 4:00 P.M., wagonloads of Confederate wounded were bouncing south on the rutted roads to Corinth. The Yankees cheered themselves hoarse when they realized the enemy were retreating.

The Union army had triumphed. By refusing to quit, they had won the Battle of Shiloh, the bloodiest battle ever fought in America up to that time. General Grant later remembered, "I saw an open field . . . so covered with dead that it would have been possible to walk across the clearing, in any direction, stepping on dead bodies, without a foot

Retreat of the Confederate army from the battleground of Shiloh to Corinth, Mississippi

touching the ground." In the two-day fight, about 13,000 Union and about 11,000 Confederate soldiers were killed, wounded, or captured. Burial details walked the littered battlefield for days stacking bodies and digging mass graves.

News of the defeat in the Tennessee woods stunned the Confederacy. So many brave Rebels had been slaughtered in their fateful quest for glory, yet they had failed to turn back the advancing Yankee tide in the West. Years later, New Orleans writer George Washington Cable sadly remembered, "The South never smiled again after Shiloh."

Many Northerners gasped at the bloody cost of victory. Some shocked politicians demanded that Ulysses S. Grant be relieved of duty. They insisted the general should have retreated early and saved his men from needless bloodshed. "I can't spare this man," President Lincoln finally responded to Grant's critics. "He fights!"

Grant was a man who learned from his experiences. He was never again taken by surprise in battle, and at Shiloh, Grant had learned that only the cruelest kind of fighting would win the Civil War. Three more years of horrible battles lay ahead. But on April 9, 1865, General Grant accepted the final surrender of Confederate general Robert E. Lee at Appomattox Court House, Virginia.

Lee (right, at table) and Grant meet at Appomattox Court
House. A newspaper (below left) announces the end of the war.
Lee's letter to Grant (below right) asked for terms of surrender.

EXTRA.

Surrender
of Lee

AND   30,000   MEN.

Peace in 6 Days

WASHINGTON, April 9, 10 P. M.
A dispatch from Secretary Stanton
to Gen. Dix says:

A dispatch from Gen. Grant announces the surrender of Gen. Lee with 30,-
000 men.

Lee would not surrender to Sheridan,
but rode furiously and successfully for
an interview with Grant, to whom he
surrendered, and was accorded the hon-
ors and privileges of a prisoner of war.
Peace will undoubtedly be declared
within six days.

9 ~ Apl '15

Genl
I have recd your note
of this date. Though not enter
taining the opinion you express
of the hopelessness of further resis
-tance on the part of the Army
of N. Va — I reciprocate your
desire to avoid useless effusion
of blood, I therefore before Consider
ing your proposition ask
the terms you will offer on
Condition of its Surrender
Very respt your Obt Srvt
R E Lee
Genl

Lt Genl U. S. Grant
Commd Armies of the U. States

INDEX

About the Author

Zachary Kent grew up in Little Falls, New Jersey, and received an English degree from St. Lawrence University. Following college he worked at a New York City literary agency for two years and then launched his writing career. To support himself while writing, he has worked as a taxi driver, a shipping clerk, and a house painter. Mr. Kent has had a lifelong interest in American history. Studying the U.S. presidents was his childhood hobby. His collection of presidential items includes books, pictures, and games, as well as several autographed letters.

3 2005 0175589 0   ial Library
                        rk 14750

J 973.731 K
Kent, Zachary.
   The story of the Battle of
Shiloh

ATE DUE   9.95

J 973.731 K
Kent, Zachary.
   The story of the Battle of
Shiloh
                              9.95

DATE DUE	BORROWER'S NAME date	ROOM NO.

WITHDRAWN
LAKEWOOD, NEW YORK 14750

Member Of
Chautauqua-Cattaraugus Library System